PUG JOKE BOOK

SECOND EDITION

BY
MOMO J PUG

ILLUSTRATED BY
JAC LAHAV

WWW.PUGJOKES.COM

WHERE DO PUGS
PARK THEIR CARS?

IN THE BARKING LOT!

WHY DO PUGS RUN IN CIRCLES?
'CAUSE IT'S REALLY HARD TO RUN IN SQUARES!
DEDICATION
THIS BOOK IS FOR MY HOOMANS WHO GIVE ME FOOD AND SNUGGLES.

WHAT DID THE PUG SAY TO THE GARDEN?
LETTUCE EAT!
A PUG BREEDER HAS 196 PUGS IN HIS YARD
BUT WHEN HE ROUNDED THEM UP, HE HAD 200!

A PUG FARTED
IN AN ELEVATOR
1 2 3
4 5 6
7 8 9
10 11 12
14 15 16
FART
EMERGENCY
IT WAS WRONG
ON SO MANY LEVELS

TWO OLD PUGS
ARE IN THE LIBRARY.
ONE LEANS OVER
AND WHISPERS

"I JUST LET OUT
A LONG, SILENT FART!
WHAT SHOULD I DO?"

THE OTHER REPLIES,
"FIRST OFF, REPLACE THE
BATTERIES IN YOUR
HEARING AID"

WHY DO PUG
FARTS SMELL?

FOR THE BENEFIT OF PEOPLE
WHO ARE
HEARING IMPAIRED!

A PUG, A KING CHARLES,
AND A POMERANIAN
WERE ALL LOST IN THE
DESERT WHEN THEY
FOUND A MAGIC LAMP!
A GENIE POPPED OUT AND
GRANTED THEM EACH ONE WISH.

THE POMERANIAN WISHED
SHE WAS BACK HOME.
POOF!
SHE WAS BACK HOME.

THE KING CHARLES WISHED
SHE WAS WITH HER FAMILY.
POOF,
SHE WAS BACK HOME
WITH HER FAMILY.

THE PUG SAID,
"AWWWWW, I WISH MY
FRIENDS WERE HERE"

WHY DO
PUG VAMPIRES
BELIEVE EVERYTHING
YOU TELL THEM?

BECAUSE
THEY'RE SUCKERS

WHAT DO YOU GET WHEN
YOU CROSS A PUG
WITH A COMPUTER?

A LOT OF LITTLE BYTES.

WHAT'S A PUGS
FAVORITE PIZZA?

PUPPERONI

WHAT KIND OF PUGS
DONT LIKE PIZZA?

WEIR-DOUGHS!

WHAT'S THE
DIFFERENCE
BETWEEN A PIZZA
AND THESE
PIZZA PUG JOKES?

PIZZA PUG JOKES
CAN'T BE TOPPED!

OK, OK, ONE MORE
PIZZA PUG JOKE...

NAH, NEVER MIND,
IT'S TOO CHEESY!

WHY DON'T
PUGS WRITE WITH
DULL PENCILS?

BECAUSE
IT'S POINTLESS

HOW DID
THE PUG
FEEL AFTER
SEEING THE
NEW SCOTTISH
DOG MOVIE?

TERRIER-FIED!

WHAT KIND OF PUG EATS WITH HIS EARS?
THEY ALL DO.
I HAVEN'T SEEN A SINGLE PUG REMOVE THEIR EARS BEFORE DINNER.
WHAT DO PUGS CALL EMPTY JARS OF CHEESE WHIZ?
CHEESE WAS

A PUG,
A KING CHARLES,
AND A DACHSHUND
WALK INTO A PIZZA PARLOUR.
THEY PROCEED TO EACH
BUY A SLICE.
JUST AS THEY'RE ABOUT
TO ENJOY THEIR YUMMY TREAT
A FLY LANDS ON
EACH OF THEIR SLICES
BECOMING STUCK IN THE
THICK MELTED CHEESE.

THE KING CHARLES
PUSHES HIS SLICE AWAY
IN DISGUST.

THE DACHSHUND FISHES
THE FLY OUT OF THE CHEESE
AND EATS IT,
SCHLURP!

THE PUG ALSO PICKS THE FLY
OUT OF HIS SLICE,
HOLDS IT OVER THE PLATE
AND STARTS YELLING
"SPIT IT OUT! SPIT IT OUT!"

WHOSE BIGGER
MR. BIGGER THE PUG
OR
MR. BIGGER'S BABY?

THE BABY
CAUSE SHE'S A LITTLE BIGGER

THE PUG WAS
SO SHOCKED FROM SEEING
HIS FIRST SHIP WRECK

HE HAD TO
LET IT
SINK IN

WHAT KIND OF
PUG MEDITATES
ON THE FULL MOON?

AWARE-WOLF!

WHAT HAPPENS
WHEN A PUG
RUNS OVER A FROG?

HE GETS TOAD!

HOW DO YOU GET A PUG TO STOP BARKING
IN THE BACK SEAT WHEN YOUR DRIVING?

LET HIM BARK IN THE FRONT SEAT!

A PUG OWNER
COMES HOME FROM
THE INTERNATIONAL MARKET

"HERE BOY!
YOU WANT
SOME BRAZILIAN TREATS?"

THE PUG REPLIES

"OH MY GOD!
I'M SO LUCKY!!!
...
WAIT...
HOW MANY IS A
BRAZILIAN?"

I TOOK MY PUG
TO THE VET.

SHE SAID
"YOUR PUG IS OVERWEIGHT"

I TOLD HER
"I WANT A SECOND OPINION!"

SHE REPLIED
"HE'S ALSO PRETTY CUTE!"

THE PUG WAS
FEELING
LOW SELF ESTEEM

"I LOOK FAT"
SHE SAID TO
THE KING CHARLES
"CAN YOU GIVE ME
A COMPLIMENT?"

THE KING CHARLES REPLIED
"YOU'VE GOT PERFECT EYESIGHT"

WHY DID THE VEGETARIAN PUG BLUSH?

HE SAW THE SALAD DRESSING

WHEN DO PUGS SAY "MOO"?

WHEN THEY LEARN A NEW LANGUAGE!

WHAT DID THE PUG SAY WAS ON TOP OF THE HOUSE?

DA ROOF ROOF ROOF!

WHAT'S A PUGS
FAVORITE
MUSICAL
INSTRUMENT?

THE DINNER BELL

WHAT'S A PUGS
SECOND FAVORITE
INSTRUMENT?

A TROM BONE!

BUT DID YOU
HEAR ABOUT
THE PUG WHO
PLAYED PIANO?

HIS BACH
WAS WORSE
THAN HIS BITE!

MY PUG IS
IN SHAPE

UNFORTUNATELY
IT'S THE
WRONG ONE

MY PUG
WAS SO FAT

HE TURNED
INTO A HUSKY!

A MAN TAKES HIS PUG
TO THE VET AND SAYS,
"MY DOG'S CROSS-EYED,
IS THERE ANYTHING YOU CAN DO FOR HIM?"

"WELL," SAYS THE VET,
"LET'S HAVE A LOOK AT HIM."
SO HE PICKS UP THE PUG
AND EXAMINES HIS EYES,
THEN CHECKS HIS TEETH.
FINALLY, HE SAYS
"I'M GOING TO HAVE TO
PUT HIM DOWN."

"WHAT? BECAUSE HE'S CROSS-EYED?"

"NO, BECAUSE HE'S REALLY HEAVY."

WHAT DID THE
PUG SAY
AFTER EATING
AT THE DALMATIAN
RESTAURANT?

THAT REALLY HIT THE SPOT!

THAT PUG
IS A REALLY
MEAN COOK!

HE WHIPS
THE CREAM
AND
BEATS THE EGGS

HOW CAN YOU
TELL IF A PUG
IS A GOOD COOK?

HE MAKES GREAT
USE OF HIS THYME!

A MAN WENT
TO VISIT A FRIEND
AND WAS
AMAZED TO FIND
HIM PLAYING CHESS
WITH HIS PUG.

HE WATCHED THE GAME
IN ASTONISHMENT
FOR A WHILE.

"I CAN HARDLY BELIEVE MY EYES!"
HE EXCLAIMED.
"THAT PUGS
THE SMARTEST DOG
I'VE EVER SEEN."

"NAH,
HE'S NOT
SO SMART,"
THE FRIEND REPLIED.

"I'VE BEATEN HIM
THREE GAMES
OUT OF FIVE."

WHAT DID THE PUG SAY TO THE TREE?
BARK!
WHAT DO YOU CALL A PUG IN A TREE WITH A BRIEFCASE?
BRANCH MANAGER

WHILE AT A
DOGGY DINNER PARTY
A PUG FARTS.

THE
KING CHARLES SAYS
"HOW DARE YOU
FART IN FRONT OF ME!"

THE PUG REPLIES
"I'M SORRY,
I DIDN'T REALIZE
IT WAS YOUR TURN!"

MY PUG IS DEPRESSED

HOW DO YOU KNOW?

EVERY TIME
I ASK HOW HIS LIFE'S GOING,
ALL HE SAYS IS
"RUFF!"

SOMEONE STOLE
MY PUG
MOOD RING!

I HAVE NO IDEA
HOW I FEEL
ABOUT IT!

KNOCK KNOCK
WHOSE THERE

DOORBELL
REPAIR PUG!

HOW DO PUG
ASTRONAUGHTS
ORGANIZE
SPACE PARTIES?

THEY PLANET!

WHEN DO PUGS
JUMP ON
TRAMPOLINES?

IN SPRING!

WHATS MORE
AMAZING THAN
A TALKING PUG?

A SPELLING BEE!

WHY DO
PUGS ALWAYS
WORK AS BAKERS?

FOR THE
EXTRA DOUGH!

WHAT DOES A PUG
EAT BEFORE
THE BIG RACE?
NOTHING.
THEY FAST
PUG PUG PUG
WHERE DID
THE PUG PARK
HIS CAR?
IN THE
BARKING LOT!

WHY DID THE PUG
ROLL TOILET PAPER
DOWN THE HILL

SO IT COULD
GET TO THE BOTTOM

WHERE DID THE PUG GO
WHEN HIS
TAIL FELL OFF?

THE RETAIL STORE!

WHAT HAPPENS
WHEN THE PUG ATE A CLOVE
OF GARLIC?

HIS BARK
WAS WORSE THAN HIS BITE!

WHATS A PUGS FAVORITE COMEDIAN?

GROWL-CHO MARX

ONE PUG
AND FOUR CATS
ARE IN A BOAT
THE PUG JUMPED OUT.
WHO IS LEFT IN THE BOAT?

NOBODY,
THEY WERE ALL
COPYCATS!

WHAT HAPPENED
WHEN THE CAT WON
THE PUG
BEAUTY CONTEST?

IT WAS A
CAT-HAS-TROPHY

WHAT DID
THE WINNER SAY?

CHECK
MEEEE-OUWT!

WHAT DO YOU GET
WHEN YOU CROSS A PUG
AND A HYENA?

I DON'T KNOW,
BUT IF IT LAUGHS, GIVE HIM A TREAT.

WHATS THE DIFFERENCE BETWEEN
A PUG AND A MARINE BIOLOGIST?

ONE WAGS A TALE,
THE OTHER
TAGS A WHALE!

WHATS THE DIFFERENCE
BETWEEN MY PUG AND A PIZZA?

(DON'T KNOW)

IN THAT CASE, I'LL BE
ORDERING DINNER TONIGHT!

A PUG AT A
BASEBALL GAME KEPT WONDERING
WHY THE BALL WAS GETTING
BIGGER
AND BIGGER AND BIGGER.

THEN IT HIT HIM!

WHAT DO YOU MEAN,
MY PUG CHASED A GUY ON A BIKE?

MY PUG DOESN'T EVEN OWN A BIKE!

DID YOU HEAR
ABOUT THE PUG WHO HAD
NO NOSE?

I HEARD HE SMELLED
AWFUL!

WHAT DO YOU CALL
A PUG WITH A FEVER?

A HOT DOG!

WHAT ABOUT A COLD PUG?

A PUPSICLE

AND IF THAT PUG
GETS EVEN COLDER?

THAT'S A CHILI DOG!

WAIT! THAT COLD
PUG IS SITTING ON A RABBIT!

OH, THAT'S
A CHILI DOG ON A BUN!

WHAT DO MY PUG
AND MY PHONE HAVE IN COMMON?

THEY BOTH
HAVE COLLAR ID

THE PUG TOLD HIS GIRLFRIEND
SHE DREW HER EYEBROWS
WAY TOO HIGH

SHE LOOKED VERY SURPRISED!

WHAT HAPPENED
WHEN THE PUG WENT
TO A FLEA CIRCUS?

HE STOLE THE SHOW

WHERE DO PUGS HATE TO SHOP?

THE FLEA MARKET!

DID YOU HEAR
ABOUT THE SPECIAL AT
THE PET STORE?

BUY 1 DOG
GET ONE FLEA!

A PUG WALKS INTO A BAR
ORDERS A DRINK.
AND SUDDENLY HE HEARS
SOMEONE SHOUTS "HEY CUTIE!"
THE PUG LOOKS AROUND BUT
NO ONE IS THERE
"HEY! NICE CURLY TAIL!"
THE PUG LOOKS UP AGAIN
BUT NOBODY'S THERE.
"HEY! CUTE TONGUE!"
THE PUG FRUSTRATED
CALLS OVER THE BARTENDER ASKING
"HEY, YOU TALKIN TO ME?".
THE BARTENDER REPLIES
"IT'S NOT ME!
IT'S THE COMPLIMENTARY PEANUTS"

A PUG IS ON A BEACH
WATCHING A HIPPIE
DROWN IN THE WATER!

THE LIFEGUARD SAYS
"AREN'T YOU GONNA
DO SOMETHING?"

THE PUG REPLIES
"NO WAY,
HE'S TOO FAR OUT"

A PUG THINKS
"WOW,
HUMANS BRING ME FOOD EVERY DAY,
THEY LET ME LIVE
IN A AWESOME HOUSE,
IT'S NOT COLD, NO RAIN,
THEY TAKE CARE OF ME...
HUMANS MUST BE GODS!"

A CAT THINKS
"WOW, HUMANS BRING ME FOOD EVERY DAY,
I LIVE IN THEIR AWESOME HOUSE,
IT'S NOT COLD, NO RAIN,
THEY TAKE CARE OF ME...
I MUST BE GOD!"

ABOUT THE AUTHOR

PUG JOKES WAS WRITTEN
BY MOMO J PUG

MOMO IS A ONE EYED PUG FROM BROOKLYN NY
SHE LOVES TREATS,
SNUGGLES, PIZZA,
TELLING JOKES
AND WRITING BOOKS!

IF YOU ENJOYED PUG JOKES
PLEASE CHECK OUT
MOMO'S OTHER TITLES
————————

ONE TRICKY PUG
THE TALE OF A SASSY PUG, AND PIZZA!

POOPIE AND THE BIG IDEA
THE POOP EMOJI BOOK

Made in the USA
Columbia, SC
20 November 2018